Harcourt Health and Fitness

Activity Book
Grade 1

Harcourt
SCHOOL PUBLISHERS

Orlando • Austin • New York • San Diego • Toronto • London

Visit *The Learning Site!*
www.harcourtschool.com

ISBN 0-15-339067-0

2 3 4 5 6 7 8 9 10 073 13 12 11 10 09 08 07 06 05

Contents

Name _____

You Are Growing

Lesson 1 pp. 4–7

Draw a line from the sense to its body part.

touch

sight

smell

hearing

taste

Lesson 2 pp. 8–9

Mark an X on the picture that does NOT show how the baby will **grow** and change.

Lesson 3 pp. 10–11

Write the letter of the word to complete each sentence.

a. muscles   **b.** bones

1. _____   Your skeleton is made up of _____.

2. _____   Some _____ help you move.

Chapter 1 • You Are Growing

Lesson 4 pp. 12–13

Draw lines to match each sentence with a word.

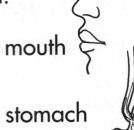

What gives your body energy?   mouth

Where do you start to digest food?   stomach

Where is food broken down?   food

Lesson 5 pp. 14–15

Use  BLUE to color
the body parts that take in air.

Use RED to color
the body parts that take what
the body needs from the air.

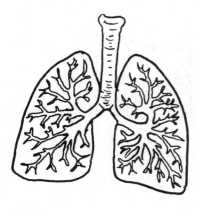

Lesson 6 pp. 16–17

Look at the picture. Then answer each question.

heart   exercise

_____
- - - - - - - - -
Which body part pumps blood? _____

_____
- - - - - - - - -
What makes the heart strong? _____

© Harcourt

Name _____

Make Predictions

Read the sentence in the first box.
Draw a picture to show what will happen.

Mario plants a seed and takes good care of it.

What Will Happen

© Harcourt

Set Goals

Steps for Setting Goals

1. Set a goal.

2. Make a plan to meet the goal.

3. Work toward the goal.

4. Ask yourself how you are doing.

Use the steps to solve this problem.

You want your heart and lungs to be healthy. Make an exercise plan. Draw pictures to show the steps you will take to meet your goal.

1.	**2.**
3.	**4.**

© Harcourt

AB **Vocabulary Reinforcement**

Hidden Word

Use the clues to fill in the missing letters.

1. ske⬭eton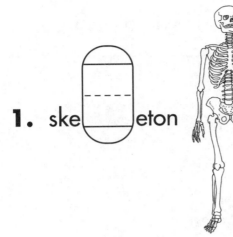

2. m⬭scles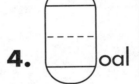

3. se⬭ses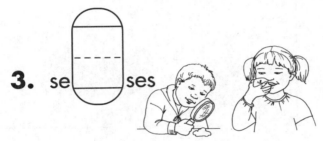

4. ⬭oal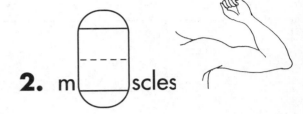

5. dige⬭t

Read the letters in the circles in order.
Use the letters to answer the question.

What body part do you use to breathe?

____ ____ ____ ____ ____

6. ____ ____ ____ ____ ____ ____

Taking Care of Your Body

Lesson 1 pp. 26–29

Draw two things you can use to keep your skin healthy.

Lesson 2 pp. 30–33

What do these clues tell about? Write the word in the web.

They help you choose the best products.

They tell you how products are alike and different.

_____
- - - - - - - -
_____

They tell you what the products do.

They tell you what is in the products.

Lesson 3 pp. 34–35

What can you do to find health information?
Write the letter of the picture that goes with
each sentence.

a.

b.

c.

_____ **1.** I can talk to a parent, doctor, or nurse.

_____ **2.** I can look in a book.

_____ **3.** I can watch a video.

© Harcourt

Name _____

Use Context Clues

sunburn   ad   sunscreen

What do these clues tell about? Write the word
in the circle.

1.

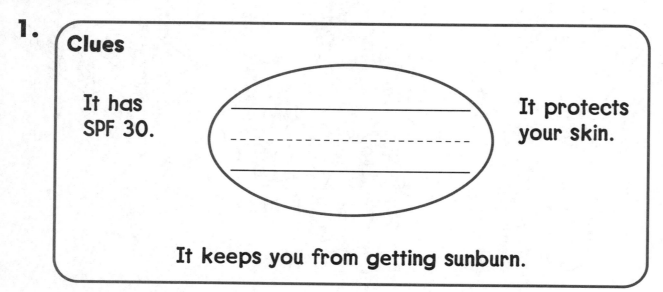

Clues

It has
SPF 30.

It protects
your skin.

It keeps you from getting sunburn.

Write two clues that tell about the word in
the circle.

2.

Clues

_____

- -

_____

(ad)

_____

- -

_____

© Harcourt

Set Goals

Steps for Setting Goals

1. Set a goal.

2. Make a plan to meet the goal.

3. Work toward the goal.

4. Ask yourself how you are doing.

Use the steps to solve this problem.

You want to keep your hands clean. Your goal is to wash your hands before and after every meal. Write sentences to tell how you will meet this goal.

_____

- -

_____

- -

_____

- -

_____

- -

_____

© Harcourt

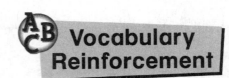

What Am I?

Write the word from the box that fits each clue.

| sunscreen | ad | sunburn | germs |

I make skin red and sore.

_____

- -

_____

We are tiny things that can make you sick.

_____

- -

_____

I protect skin from the sun.

_____

- -

_____

I try to get you to buy a product.

_____

- -

_____

CHAPTER 3

Name _____

Your Teeth

Lesson 1 pp. 44–47

Write a word or words from the box to complete each sentence.

| primary teeth | bite | permanent teeth | chew |

_____

Your _____ grow in when you are a baby.

Your back teeth help you _____ food into small pieces.

Your _____ are your second set of teeth.

You _____ into food with your front teeth.

Lesson 2 pp. 48–51

Draw two times when you should brush your teeth.

Lesson 3 | pp. 54–55

Circle the picture that shows a way to keep your teeth safe. Cross out the picture that shows something that can harm your teeth.

Lesson 4 | pp. 56–57

What are two reasons you visit the **dentist**?

_____

_____

_____

_____

_____

_____

Sequence

Use sequencing to number the pictures in order.
Write 1, 2, or 3 below each picture.

_____

- - - - - - -

_____

_____

- - - - - - -

_____

_____

- - - - - - -

_____

_____

- - - - - - -

_____

- - - - - - -

_____

- - - - - - -

© Harcourt

Problem Solving

Resolve Conflicts

Steps for Resolving Conflicts

1. Agree that there is a problem.

2. Listen to each other.

3. Think of ways to work together.

4. Find a way for both sides to win.

Use the steps to solve this problem.

You and a friend want to play with a toy that is still in the package. Your friend wants to rip the package open with his teeth. He starts to do it. You know this is not a good idea. You get mad at him. How do you resolve the conflict?

_____

- -

_____

_____

- -

_____

_____

- -

_____

_____

- -

_____

Name _____

Tooth Mystery

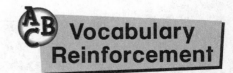
Vocabulary Reinforcement

> **permanent teeth**   **dentist**   **primary teeth**
> **dental hygienist**   **floss**

Write the words from the box to complete each sentence.

_____

A _____ fixes
tooth problems.

_____

Your _____ are
your first set of teeth.

_____

A _____ helps
a dentist clean your teeth.

_____

You use _____
to clean between your teeth.

_____

Your _____ are
your second set of teeth.

© Harcourt

Name _____

Wonderful Food

Lesson 1 pp. 64–65

Draw two pictures of ways you use energy.

Lesson 2 pp. 66–69

Draw lines from the food groups to their correct
places on the **Food Guide Pyramid**.

vegetables

milk, yogurt,
cheese

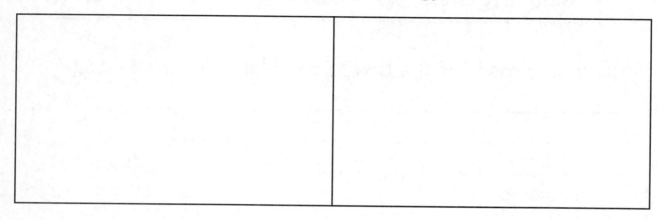

fats, oils, sweets

breads, cereals,
rice, pasta

fruits

meat, poultry,
fish, dried beans,
eggs, nuts

Lesson 3 pp. 70–73

Fill in the missing vowels.

br____ ____kf____st   d____nn____r

Lesson 4 pp. 76–77

Write or draw your own ad for cereal.

Lesson 5 pp. 78–79

Fill in the web.

Detail
_____
- - - - - - - - - - -
Wash _____
and vegetables
before you eat them.

Detail
Wash your hands
with soap and
_____
- - - - - - - - - - - -
_____.

Main Idea
You can
help keep
food safe.

Detail
Some foods such as
_____
- - - - - - - - - - - -
_____,
eggs, juice, and meat
need to stay cold.

Detail
_____
- - - - - - - - - - - -
_____
foods and put
them away.

© Harcourt

Find the Main Idea

Eating meals and snacks gives you energy. A good breakfast gives your body the energy it needs to start the day. A good lunch and dinner help your body have energy all day long. Snacks give you extra energy for work and play.

Detail

_____

- - - - - - - - - - - - - - - -

_____ gives your body energy at the start of the day.

Detail

_____

- - - - - - - - - - - - - - - -

_____ give you extra energy for work and play.

Main Idea

Eating meals and snacks _____

- - - - - - - - - - - - - - - -

gives you _____ .

Detail

_____   _____

- - - - - - - - - - - -   - - - - - - - - - - - -

_____ and _____ give your body energy all day.

© Harcourt

Make Decisions

Steps for Making Decisions

1. Think about the choices.

2. Say NO to choices that are against your family rules.

3. Ask yourself what could happen with each choice.

4. Make the best choice.

Use the steps to solve this problem.

You want a snack. You see cookies, a can of soda, and an apple. You know your parents want you to choose healthful foods. What will you choose? Tell why.

_____

_____

_____

_____

_____

_____

_____

© Harcourt

Name _____

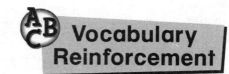
Food Words

Draw a line to match each word with its meaning.

Words	**Meanings**
1. breakfast	**a.** a meal eaten around noon
2. snack	**b.** a meal eaten in the evening
3. lunch	**c.** the first meal of the day
4. dinner	**d.** food eaten between meals

Choose one word from the list of words above.
Write a sentence that uses that word.

_____

- -

_____

- -

_____

- -

_____

Draw a picture for your sentence.

CHAPTER 5

Name _____

Keeping Active

Lesson 1 pp. 86–87

Does this boy have good posture?
Tell how you know.

_____

- - - - - - - - - - - - - - - - - - - -

_____

_____

- - - - - - - - - - - - - - - - - - - -

_____

_____

- - - - - - - - - - - - - - - - - - - -

Lesson 2 pp. 88–91

Draw three ways you can stay fit.

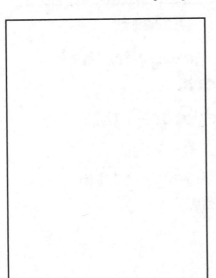
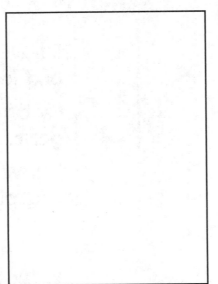

Lesson 3 pp. 94–97

Write the word from the box that best
completes the sentence.

| water | helmet | stretch |

_____

To _____ is to gently pull your muscles.

For some kinds of exercise, you may need

_____

a _____ and pads to stay safe.

_____

Drink lots of _____ when you exercise.

Lesson 4 pp. 98–99

Read these effects. Write or draw to tell their cause.

Cause		**Effects**
		I have energy to think and learn. My body can fight germs. I have energy to run and play.

© Harcourt

Find Cause and Effect

Write or draw to tell a cause for this effect.

Cause

Effect

I stay safe when
I exercise.

→

Name _____

Manage Stress

Steps for Managing Stress

1. Know what stress feels like.

2. Think about what is making you feel stress.

3. Do something that will help you feel better.

4. Get exercise.

Use the steps to solve this problem.

You are going to sing in the school concert tomorrow. You are worried that you will make a mistake. What can you do to manage your stress?

_____

- -

_____

- -

_____

- -

_____

- -

© Harcourt

Picture Fitness

Write a sentence for
each set of pictures.

physical fitness

_____

- -

_____

- -

_____

- -

_____

stretch

_____

- -

_____

- -

_____

- -

_____

CHAPTER 6

Name _____

Being Safe

Lesson 1 pp. 106–109

Write **Do** or **Do not** to complete each safety rule.

_____ touch hot things.

_____ put your things away.

_____ call 911 in an emergency.

_____ climb up a slide.

Lesson 2 pp. 110–113

Draw two pictures to show how to stay safe in a car or on a bus.

Lesson 3 pp. 114–117

Write a word from the box below each picture.

Think   Stop   Listen   Look

_____ _____ _____ _____

- - - - - - - - -   - - - - - - - - -   - - - - - - - - -   - - - - - - - - -

_____ _____ _____ _____

Lesson 4 pp. 118–121

Write a fire safety rule to go with this picture.

_____

- -

_____

Lesson 5 pp. 124–125

Look at the picture. What should the girl do to be safe in the boat?

_____

- - - - - - - - - - - - - - - - - -

_____ in a boat.

_____

- - - - - - - - - - - - - - - - -

Wear a _____ .

Sequence

Write the number below the boxes to show the sequence. Then draw pictures to show the step. Write the step under each picture.

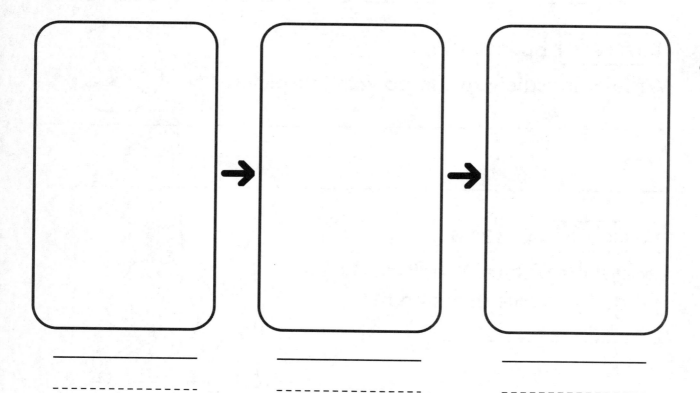

| **Roll.** Roll over on the ground. | → | **Drop.** Lie down. Cover your face. | → | **Stop.** Do not run or wave your arms. |

© Harcourt

Refuse

Steps for Refusing

1. Say NO, and tell why.

2. Think about what could happen.

3. Suggest something else to do.

4. Say NO again, and walk away.

Use the steps to solve this problem.

You are at the playground. Your friend wants you to jump off a swing. What will you do? Tell why.

_____

- -

_____

_____

- -

_____

_____

- -

_____

_____

- -

_____

Safety Matching

Draw a line to match each vocabulary word with the correct picture.

1. emergency

a.

2. playground equipment

b.

3. safety belt

c.

4. crosswalk

d.

Quick Study

Avoiding Danger

Lesson 1 pp. 132–133

Use the words from the box to complete the sentences in the web.

name   strangers   NO   door

Detail
Do not go anywhere
_____
- - - - - - - - - - - - - - -
with _____.

Detail
Never tell strangers
_____
- - - - - - - - - - - - - - -
your _____ or
where you live.

Main Idea
A stranger can put
you in danger.

Detail
Do not open the
_____
- - - - - - - - - - - - - - -
_____ to
strangers.

Detail
If a stranger bothers you,
_____
- - - - - - - - - - - - - - -
say _____, get
away, and tell someone.

© Harcourt

Chapter 7 • Avoiding Danger

Lesson 2 pp. 136–137

Write or draw a warning
label for insect spray
that has **poison** in it.

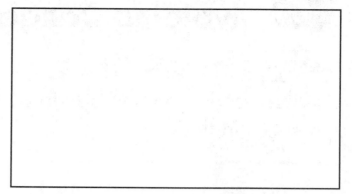

Lesson 3 pp. 138–139

Write the word from the box that best completes
the sentence.

| weapons | police officer | touch |

_____

Guns and knives are _____.

Never _____ a weapon.

If you see a weapon, tell a parent, _____,
or teacher.

© Harcourt

Recall and Retell

Recall the details. Retell what you learned about staying safe from strangers.

Recall Detail
1. Do not talk to a stranger.

Retell

Recall Detail
2. Do not go with a stranger.

Recall Detail
3. Say NO, run away, and tell a trusted adult about a stranger.

© Harcourt

Communicate

Steps for Communicating

1. Decide whom to talk to.

2. Listen carefully. Answer any questions.

3. Say what you need to say.

4. Follow directions.

Use the steps to solve this problem.

You are at a parade with your mother. Your hat falls off. After you pick it up, you can not find your mother. How should you get help?

_____

- -

_____

- -

_____

- -

_____

- -

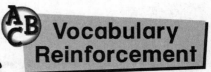

Code for Avoiding Danger

Use the number code to spell the words.

1 = a	
2 = d	
3 = e	
4 = g	
5 = i	
6 = n	
7 = o	
8 = p	
9 = r	
10 = s	
11 = t	
12 = w	

__ __ __ __ __ __

8 - 7 - 5 - 10 - 7 - 6

__ __ __ __ __ __ __

12 - 3 - 1 - 8 - 7 - 6 - 10

__ __ __ __ __ __ __ __

10 - 11 - 9 - 1 - 6 - 4 - 3 - 9

© Harcourt

Staying Well

Lesson 1 pp. 146–149

Write how you might feel if you have a cold.

_____

- -

_____

- -

_____

Lesson 2 pp. 152–155

Draw two ways you can help stop germs from spreading.

Lesson 3 pp. 156–157

Use the word **allergies** in a
sentence about the picture.

_____

- -

_____

- -

_____

© Harcourt

Lesson 4 pp. 158–159

Write a word from the box to complete each sentence.
Then answer the question.

> checkups   healthful   exercise   clean   sleep

Eat foods that are _____.

Walk, jog, or do some other _____ each day.

Keep your hands and your body _____.

Visit the doctor to get _____.

Get enough _____ every night.

What do these rules help you do? _____

Find Cause and Effect

Read the cause. Write or draw two effects this cause may have.

Cause		**Effects**

Paul has an allergy to grass. His grandfather is cutting the grass.

Communicate

Steps for Communicating

1. Decide whom to talk to.

2. Say what you need to say.

3. Listen carefully. Answer any questions.

4. Get information.

Use the steps to solve this problem.

You are at a friend's house. Your head begins to hurt. You feel tired and achy. Whom should you tell? What should you say and do?

_____

- -

_____

_____

- -

_____

_____

- -

_____

_____

- -

_____

© Harcourt

Name _____

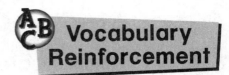
Staying Healthy Puzzle

Use the words in the box to solve the puzzle.

virus	allergy	bacteria
ill	disease	vaccines

Across

2. medicines that keep your body from getting some diseases

4. germs that can make your stomach hurt

6. an unhealthy way the body reacts because of something around you

Down

1. another word for <u>illness</u>

3. a kind of germ that causes flu

5. another word for <u>sick</u>

© Harcourt

CHAPTER 9

Name _____

About Medicines and Drugs

Quick Study

Lesson 1 pp. 166–169

Use the words in the box to finish the web.

Labels   never   safe   doctor

Detail
Keep medicines in a
_____
- - - - - - - - - - - - - - - -
_____ place.

Detail
_____
- - - - - - - - - - - - - - - -
_____ tell you
what medicines do.

Main Idea
Always use medicines safely.

Detail
_____
- - - - - - - - - - - - - - - -
You should _____
take medicines on your
own.

Detail
You need a note from a
_____
- - - - - - - - - - - - - - - -
_____ to buy
some medicines.

Lesson 2 pp. 170–171

Draw two drinks that have **caffeine**.

| | |
| | |

© Harcourt

Lesson 3 pp. 172–173

Write the correct word to
complete each sentence.

habit   legal

_____

Using tobacco is a _____ that is hard to stop.

_____

Tobacco is not _____ for children.

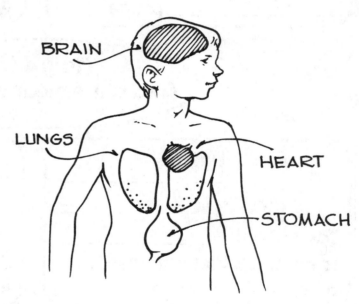

Lesson 4 pp. 174–175

Color the body parts
that can be harmed
by **alcohol**.

Lesson 5 pp. 176–177

Read each sentence. Mark an X under Yes or No.

	Yes	No
Should you take **medicine** from a friend?		
Should you tell an adult if you see **drugs**?		
Should you trust **tobacco** ads?		
Should you stay away from **tobacco smoke**?		

© Harcourt

Name _____

Find the Main Idea

Write the correct word or words from the box
to complete each detail.

tobacco smoke   Tobacco   habit   Drugs

Detail

_____

- - - - - - - - - - - - - - - - - - -

_____ in
tobacco can cause lung
disease.

Detail

_____

- - - - - - - - - - - - - - - - - - -

_____ is
not legal for children.

Main Idea
Tobacco has
drugs in it that can
harm your body.

Detail
Other people's

_____

- - - - - - - - - - - - - - - - - - -

_____ can
harm your lungs.

Detail
Using tobacco is a

_____

- - - - - - - - - - - - - - - - - - -

_____ that
harms people's health.

© Harcourt

Refuse

Steps for Refusing

1. Say NO.
Tell why not.

2. Think about what could happen.

3. Suggest something else to do.

4. Go home if you need to.

Use the steps to solve this problem.

Your friend finds a pack of cigarettes. She wants you to smoke one. How should you say NO?

_____

_____

_____

_____

_____

_____

_____

_____

© Harcourt

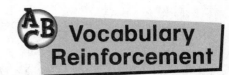

Medicines and Drugs

Write the word that goes with each picture.

| medicines | alcohol | refuse | caffeine | tobacco |

	_____
	_____
	_____
	_____

CHAPTER 10

Name _____

You Have Feelings

Quick Study

Lesson 1 pp. 186–187

Draw two pictures that show how you are **special**.

Lesson 2 pp. 188–191

Write the word that tells about each feeling.

| happy | angry | sad | afraid |

_____

- - - - - - - - - - -

_____

_____

- - - - - - - - - - -

_____

_____

- - - - - - - - - - -

_____

_____

- - - - - - - - - - -

_____

© Harcourt

Lesson 3 pp. 194–195

Write the word that best completes each sentence.

kind   talk   share   friend   help

_____

A _____ is a person you know and like.

Good friends _____ things with each other.

Good friends also _____ each other do things.

A friend is someone you can _____ to.

Good friends are _____ to each other.

Lesson 4 pp. 196–199

Look at the picture. Write about how
the children are showing **respect**.

_____

_____

_____

Use Context Clues

1. **Read the sentences. Find four clues that tell about the word in the circle. Write them.**

Good friends are kind. They share and help. They play together. They talk and listen to one another.

Clues

_____   _____
- - - - - - - - - - - - - -   - - - - - - - - - - - - - - - - -
_____   _____

(**friends**)

_____   _____
- - - - - - - - - - - - - -   - - - - - - - - - - - - - - - - -
_____   _____

2. **Use the clues to unscramble the word in the circle. Write the word.**

Clues

mad   **agrny**   shout

_____
- - - - - - - - - - - - - - - - -
_____

upset   yell

Manage Stress

Steps for Managing Stress

1. Know what stress feels like.

2. Figure out what is making you feel stress.

3. Do something that will help you feel better. Talk with someone you trust.

4. Think about doing well instead of feeling stress.

Use the steps to solve this problem.

You and your sister are going to visit your grandparents. You will be taking an airplane by yourselves. You feel stress. How should you manage your stress?

_____

- -

_____

_____

- -

_____

_____

- -

_____

_____

- -

_____

© Harcourt

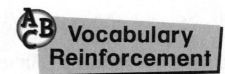

Find the Missing Words

Write the correct word to complete the sentence.
Look at the pictures for help.

special	feelings	polite	angry	respect	friends

I feel _____ when my puppy
chews up my things.

I have fun playing with my
_____

_____ .

I show _____ by listening while
others are talking.

I feel _____ when I play the
drums for my family.

I had very sad _____ when
my family moved.

To be _____, I knock on my
sister's door before going in.

© Harcourt

CHAPTER 11

Name _____

Your Family

Lesson 1 pp. 206–207

Draw two ways you can show you love and care for your family.

Lesson 2 pp. 208–209

Write <u>happy</u> or <u>sad</u> to tell how each family might feel.

A grandparent moves away.  _____	A parent comes home after being away.  _____
A baby sister is born.  _____	An older brother goes away to school. 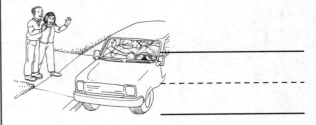 _____

© Harcourt

Lesson 3 pp. 210–213

Tell how members of each family work together.

_____

- - - - - - - - - - - - - - - - - - - -

_____

_____

- - - - - - - - - - - - - - - - - - - -

_____

_____

_____

_____

- - - - - - - - - - - - - - - - - - - -

_____

_____

- - - - - - - - - - - - - - - - - - - -

_____

_____

- - - - - - - - - - - - - - - - - - - -

_____

_____

- - - - - - - - - - - - - - - - - - - -

_____

Focus Skill **Reading Skill**

Recall and Retell

Retell what you learned about how families change.

| Recall Detail 1. A family can change in many ways. | | **Retell** |

| Recall Detail 2. A new baby can make you feel happy. | | |

| Recall Detail 3. When someone moves away, you may feel sad. | | |

Resolve Conflicts
Steps for Resolving Conflicts

1. Agree that there is a problem.

2. Listen to each other.

3. Think of ways to work together.

4. Find a way for both sides to win.

Use the steps to solve this problem.

Your grandmother gives you and your sister a new book. You both want to read it. How could you resolve this conflict?

_____

- -

_____

- -

_____

- -

_____

- -

_____

- -

_____

- -

_____

Mystery Word

Follow the directions to find the mystery word.

Write the first letter in FUN.   _____

Write the second letter in CARING.   _____

Write the first letter in MOTHER.   _____

Write the second letter in SISTER.   _____

Write the first letter in **LOVE**.   _____

Write the last letter in HAPPY.   _____

Put the letters together to make the word that names the group of people you **love**.

____ ____ ____ ____ ____ ____

____ ____ ____ ____ ____ ____

Draw a picture about this word on another piece of paper.

CHAPTER 12

Name _____

A Healthful Neighborhood

Lesson 1 pp. 222–225

Draw a line to match each **community** helper
with what he or she does.

A school nurse

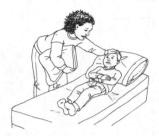

A firefighter

A doctor

A police officer

| puts out fires. |

| helps children who feel ill at school. |

| helps keep you safe. |

| finds out why you are ill. |

© Harcourt

Lesson 2 pp. 226–229

Draw an unhealthful **environment**.

How can people make the environment healthful?

_____

- -

_____

_____

- -

_____

- -

_____

Lesson 3 pp. 232–233

Read the sentence. Draw what the recycled
items could be made into.

A family recycles paper, cans, and bottles.

© Harcourt

Make Predictions

Mr. Hill calls 911 to tell about
a fire.

**Make a prediction about what
will happen next. Write or
draw your prediction.**

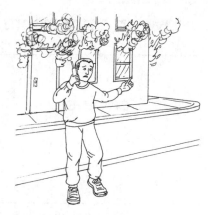

Prediction

**Read the rest of the story to find out what
happened. Then write about or draw what
happened.**

Firefighters drive a fire truck to Mr. Hill's house.
They use the hose and water to put out the fire.

What Happened

Was your prediction correct? Yes _____ No _____

Name _____

Make Decisions

Steps for Making Decisions

Problem Solving

1. Think about the choices.

2. Say NO to choices that are against the law or your family's rules.

3. Ask yourself what could happen with each choice.

4. Make the best choice.

Use the steps to solve this problem.

You eat a juice pop at the beach. Now you have a juice pop stick. What will you do with it? Tell why.

_____

- -

_____

_____

- -

_____

- -

_____

- -

_____

- -

_____

© Harcourt

Tell About the Pictures

Write two words from the box to go with
the picture.

nurse	pollution	doctor	litter

1.

_____ _____

- - - - - - - - - - - - - - - - - - - -

_____ _____

2.

_____ _____

- - - - - - - - - - - - - - - - - - - -

_____ _____

3. Use the words **recycle** and **community**
to write about the picture.

GLASS
PLASTIC
PAPER
GLASS

_____

- -

_____

- -

_____

- -

_____